Anonymous

Thoughts on Improving the Government

of the British territorial possessions in the East Indies

Anonymous

Thoughts on Improving the Government
of the British territorial possessions in the East Indies

ISBN/EAN: 9783337316013

Printed in Europe, USA, Canada, Australia, Japan

Cover: Foto ©Suzi / pixelio.de

More available books at **www.hansebooks.com**

THOUGHTS

ON

IMPROVING

THE

GOVERNMENT

OF THE

BRITISH Territorial Poſſeſſions

IN THE

EAST INDIES.

Βουλευσομεσθα, και το μεν καλως εχον
Ὅτως χρονιζον ευ μενη, Βιλευτεον.
Ὅτω δε και δει φαρμακων παιωνιων,
Ἠτι κεαντες, ἢ τεμοντες ευφρονως,
Πειρασομεσθα πηματος τρεψαι νοσον.

ÆSCHYL. in Agam.

We will conſult, that what is well may keep
Its goodneſs permanent, and what requires
Our healing hand, with mild ſeverity
May be correﬅed.

POTTER's Tranſlation.

LONDON:
Printed for T. CADELL, in the Strand.
M.DCC.LXXX.

ERRATA.

Page 55. line 25. *for* anology *read* analogy
Page 73. laſt line, for *trahitur* read *trahetur*

THOUGHTS, &c.

THE advantages which may arife from a proper adminiftration and folid arrangement of the political government of our territorial poffeffions in the Eaft Indies, have never yet met with that confideration from the legiflature which they deferve. If no other motives can induce us to think of the very great benefits which may in every view be derived from thence, our prefent exigencies at leaft may have that beneficial effect.

Three vaft provinces, full of induftry and wealth, were acquired by Lord Clive's treaty in 1775, yielding 1,650,900*l.* to the Eaft India Company, independant of a fum of 50 lacks, which were allotted to Sujah Dowla, and of Lord Clive's Jaghire. We have, befides this, the fettle-

ments

ments upon the coasts of Malabar, and Coromandel. Yet these have produced but a very inadequate benefit to this country, and are in danger of becoming less and less beneficial to us, owing to the want of due attention to the nature of such establishments, both with respect to the power which governs them at home, and the constitution of their government abroad.

The object of these few pages is to point out some of the most material defects in the administration of our affairs in the East, both at home and abroad, and to propose the method of amending them; by which the public will receive much of that advantage which now falls into the hands of individuals, and thereby becomes rather an evil than an advantage.

That all conquests or acquisitions made by subjects, either by means of arms or of negociation, belong to the sovereignty of the state, to the effect of giving the national council a right to regulate the administration of them, and of giving the public a right to participate in the advan-

tages

tages which may be derived from them, is a pofition denied by no fpeculative writer, and is directly affirmed by the law and conftitution of Great Britain. Agreeably to this principle, the legiflature has often adverted to this fubject, but till of late years the extent of its importance feems not to have been underftood, nor has it yet been fo underftood as to fuggeft the fundamental principles, which can alone fecure to us the advantage to be derived by fuch acquifitions.

The two great foundations of all national wealth, are agriculture, and commerce. In Europe the commercial fyftem has had a decided fuperiority over the agricultural, ever fince the difcovery of America, and of the paffage to India by the Cape of Good Hope. A ftrong and immediate attraction of the national capital towards the one, can never operate but at the expence of the other, and to thefe two events is in a great meafure to be afcribed, the advancement and improvement of commerce, while agriculture has been furprizingly neglected, as the face of every country in Europe will teftify, England
itfelf

itself not excepted. The opening of those vaft fources of commercial advantage to the kingdoms of Europe, roufed in a moment every avaricious principle, which lurks in the breafts of ftates, or individuals. Monopolies inftantly fprung up in every nation except the Portuguefe, and general monopolies begot individual monopolies, by much the moft deftructive of the two. It may not now be the proper time to agitate the great queftion, whether the trade from Britain to India ought to be carried on by an exclufive company or not, but it is certainly a fit time to examine the principles on which the government of our dominions in the Eaft ought to be carried on, with as much public advantage as a monopoly can admit of. If the monopoly of this trade fhall continue to be thought neceffary, yet the delegation of the powers of government needs not for that reafon to be placed in the hands of the monopolifts, but on the contrary it ought to be taken out of thofe hands, when the territories which have fprung from our trade become objects of too great magnitude, for the fuperintendance

dance of any power but that of the legiſlature.

The monopolies of the European ſtates
have been of two ſorts. The one, ex-
cluding all other nations from any commerce with its foreign dominions, of
which the Britiſh trade with America may
be taken as an example. The other, ex-
cluding all their own ſubjects, except a
favourite company, from any ſhare in the
trade to diſtant ſettlements, as in the caſe
of the Eaſt India Company. Both of theſe
monopolies are attended with very pernicious conſequences to the ſtate which adopts
them. It would be foreign to the preſent
enquiry, to examine the effects of the former, but the latter ſpecies may properly
be conſidered as expoſed to the following
obſervations. The eſtabliſhment of an
excluſive company puts all the reſt of the
ſubjects at the mercy of that company,
with reſpect to the price of every commodity which they import, and limits the
extent of the quantity of labour required
from this country, to ſupply the Eaſt,
according to the pleaſure, or the good or
ill conduct of thoſe who conduct the monopoly.

nopoly. It is, in the strictest sense of the word, a monopoly against our fellow-subjects. When any man purchases East India goods, it is obvious that he must pay, not only the original price of the commodity, together with an exorbitant profit to the company, but that he must also pay a share of the waste occasioned by the frauds and abuse necessarily connected with such an institution, and which every man knows have uniformly attended it. The spirit of monopoly, when left entirely uncontrouled, as in the Dutch Spice Islands, in a short space of time produced a compleat desolation and a destruction of the very articles of commerce which those islands produce, in order to perfect the system of monopoly. In the British dominions, the same principles have produced effects similar in their nature, and differing only in degree. An order that rice should be eradicated, to make way for a crop of opium, and *vice versâ*, when the mercantile Governor found his interest in that cruel measure, is related in the history of our administration in Bengal; and little doubt can be entertained, but

that

that we fhould have followed the Dutch example throughout, had not the legiflature at times interpofed; which proves to a demonftration the neceffity of eftablifhing an overruling authority in India, derived from the legiflature itfelf, and independant of the mercantile company. The Englifh and the Dutch have made confiderable conquefts in the Eaft, yet the fpirit of monopoly has ever crufhed the firft appearances of eftablifhed colonies, in thofe countries. It is very obvious to every attentive mind, that the flourifhing condition of foreign poffeffions, with refpect to population, manufacture, and agriculture, muft augment the quantity of labour, in that ftate which has dominion over them; and it follows *è converfo*, that a diminution of the profperity of thofe poffeffions, proportionably depreffes the quantity of labour which might be produced in return for their commodities, in the governing ftate. Another propofition is equally clear, namely, that in every country, the revenue of the fovereign, or fovereign ftate, muft be derived from that of the people. The greater the number

B   of

of that people, the greater will be the
furplus of their labour, beyond what fup-
plies their own exigencies ; and confequently the greater will be the portion
which may be fafely allotted to the fovereign, or fovereign ftate.   If this be a demonftrable or rather a felf-evident truth,
and if it be equally demonftrable, though
perhaps not equally felf-evident, that exclufive companies have a direct tendency
to counteract population, commerce, and
agriculture, the inference is irrefiftible,
that if an exclufive company be unavoid-
able, the utmoft degree of care is neceffary to obviate the ill effects of it as far
as poffible, with refpect to the SOVE-
REIGNTY.   The directors of the Eaft
India Company have evidently the fame
intereft in the good government of the
Eaft, which the ftate itfelf has ; but the
fervants of the company have no intereft
whatfoever in its permanent profperity.
The directors have therefore in general
meant well, in all their regulations, and
have been in a continual ftate of conten-
tion with their fervants, endeavouring, as
far as lay within the compafs of their
judgment,

judgment, or their powers, to reftrain the ill conduct of their agents in India. But all their efforts have been weak and inadequate. No country was ever expofed to fuch inordinate rapine by the hands of thofe who had no intereft in its exiftence, beyond the fhort term of their refidence there. The powers of the company have fcarce been able to check this rapine, though with the affiftance of the legiflature they have in a confiderable degree accomplifhed that purpofe. But the *origo mali* lies farther back. The Court of Directors, or in other words a committee of merchants, are in the nature of things unfitted for the purpofe of governing that country in which their exclufive monopoly is exercifed. The firft object with a body of profeffional men, is their profeffion. Merchandize is the firft object with merchants. Government will only be an acceffory, a mere fecondary confideration, fubfervient to its principal. To fell very dear, and to purchafe cheap by dint of authority and power, will be the natural confequence of this impolitic union of the mercantile and fovereign characters; and

temporary

temporary profit will in a great degree take place of lafting policy, even among the Directors. The mercantile character is no way fuited to the exercife of authority, nor can they maintain it in any other way than by the affiftance of military force. If this reafoning be well founded, the conclufion to be drawn from it will naturally be this; that a compleat remedy ought to be found, for the imperfections of the adminiftration of our affairs in India, at home as well as abroad. The Directors of the company are nothing more than a committee of the ftockholders, chofen from among themfelves by ballot; and when they are thus chofen, almoft the whole of the government of the Britifh intereft in India, as well as the trading concerns of the company, is committed to their charge, fubject to the review of the ftock-holders at large. The welfare of twelve millions of people, and the extent and duration of the national advantage to be derived from the trade and territorial revenue of India, reft on this foundation. Nothing furely can be more contrary to every principle of government which

which has been known among men, than
that fuch a ſtate ſhould ultimately depend upon the votes of a large number of
accidental proprietors of ſtock, men of
all deſcriptions and of all nations, who
purchaſe a ſhare in its government to-day,
and may ſell it again to-morrow. It may
I believe be ſafely aſſerted, that the government of a diſtant Empire was never
before placed in a body of men ſo fluctu-
ating in their nature, and related to the
ſubject-matter of their government by no
other tie, than that of getting a tolerable
intereſt for one or two thouſand pounds.
That the proprietors of the trading capital
ſhould manage the trade carried on with
that capital, may be right and beneficial;
and the obvious inference is, that the deliberations of thoſe perſons, when aſſembled
in their corporate capacity, ought to be
confined to that ſubject only. The Eaſt
India Company ſhould therefore be re-
ſtrained in this point, merely to what re-
gards their inveſtments and dividends;
and theſe, it is to be obſerved, were the
only ſubjects, which originally exiſted for
their determinations. This is fair political

cal ground for reftraining them, as it never can be maintained, that their powers
are to be commenfurate to every poffible
increafe of the Britifh Empire in thofe
parts. This muft be the foundation of
all good government in India, viz. that
the executive officers there, fhould be
appointed by the crown, in the fame
manner as they are directed by the conftitution to be, in our other foreign dominions; and no good reafon has ever
been given, why a difference fhould be
made in this effential point, between Afia
and America. The argument againft this
has ufually been drawn from an apprehenfion of the public danger which would
arife, from an over great extenfion of the
patronage of the crown. This anfwer
however may be given to it, namely, that
as that patronage has nearly fet in the
Weft, it may rife again in the Eaft, without any alteration in the former equili-
brium; and this more general anfwer
may alfo be given, that it is the neceffary confequence of the increafe of empire.
If it is an evil, it is the fmaller evil of
the two; and the common adage will here
give

give us a right and folid conclufion, that of two evils we muſt chuſe the leaſt. Reaſon and paſt experience (which in politics is the furer guide of the two) both concur in ſettling this point; but as it may be doubted by men of democratic perſuaſions, ſome other arguments may have weight in this conſideration, derived from the nature of the country itſelf.

The great Peninſula of India is a conquered country, parcelled out among Mahometan tyrants, and thoſe few native Princes who remain in poſſeſſion of their original territories. This creates two hereditary parties. The native princes juſtly abhor the Mahometans. They are of a peaceful, laborious, patient character, and a juſt and gentle government eſtabliſhed there, they are ſenſible would be a comfort and protection to them. The Mahometan princes are humiliated and galled with the thought of being under the ſway of a company of merchants, and have turned their eyes towards the crown of theſe realms, ever ſince they acquired a knowledge of the nature of the Britiſh government. The caprice of the company's

pany's government, added to all the rapine
that has attended it, has made it odious
to an extreme. All this paves the way to
a change beneficial to the public. I fay
beneficial, becaufe it would fatisfy and
reconcile to us the natives of Indoftan.
The politics of thofe princes, are exactly
of a nature refulting from fuch a ftate of
government as they have hitherto lived
under; they confift of intrigue, artifice,
fufpicion, and all crafty methods of getting materials to guide their conduct, by
means of fpies, corruption, &c. and du-
plicity becomes of courfe their favourite
plan. Fear and jealoufy compel the natives, to return to the bowels of the earth
the precious metals which were originally extracted from them; yet by a wife
conduct thefe might be turned to a better
ufe, as fhall hereafter be fhewn.

· All this and much more has certainly·
arifen, from an undignified, unfteady,
mercantile government carried on by monopolifts; much of it therefore might be
done away, by eftablifhing a national government there, to which fome late regulations have tended. According to the
habitual

habitual opinion of Afiatics, it is a matter of importance that they fhould confider themfelves as connected with the Supreme Power in that ftate to which they are fu-bordinate; the whole current of their ideas having flowed in that courfe, they will with pleafure bend themfelves in fubjection to officers appointed by the Sovereign who reprefents that ftate; being fully apprifed of the comparative dignity of fuch an appointment, and that of a fuperior appointed under the feal of the company. It will be fhewn too in the fequel, that the number of appointments to be vefted in the crown is but fmall, and fuch as needs not reafonably to be alarming to thofe, who have a dread of increafing the power of that member of our conftitution. It will fuffice, and amply fuffice, if a few of the principal officers are appointed by the crown; for the government of any diftant country under the ultimate controul of parliament, ought not to be placed in many hands.

Taking it then as clear that the territorial poffeffions in India fhould be deemed (to all purpofes of civil government) a

part

part of the Britifh Empire, and as fuch to
be governed with the fame view to public
benefit that other conquefts and acquifitions are ; we are now to confider the objects which moft require a legiflative cor-
rection, and the manner in which the
civil government ought to be carried on.
It feems to be the opinion of all men, that
fomething extenfive, permanent, and ra-
dical muft now be done, in order to ar-
range matters in fuch a manner, as that
all poffible affiftance may be derived from
that country to aid us in our prefent difficulties, and be a fund for enabling us to
bear thofe which may hereafter arife.
The expiration of the company's charter,
and the decided preponderance of the Britifh influence in India, added to every
motive which can arife from a confcioufnefs of paft neglect, abfolutely require
that the conductors of public bufinefs
fhould advert moft ferioufly to this vaft
object. We who live under governments
long eftablifhed, grounded upon wife
principles, and gradually brought to a
wonderful degree of perfection, are fo
much accuftomed to contemplate thofe
princi-

principles in a familiar manner, that we think it trite or pedantic to repeat them: but when we find that thefe principles have never yet been applied to the government of the Eaft, it is plain we re-quire to be reminded of them. One of thefe principles is, that in proportion as a fubordinate territory is well or ill governed, in fuch proportion exactly will it be productive and beneficial to the fuperior ftate. If this be a pofition generally true, with what force does it apply to a country, once crouded with peaceful manufacturers and hufbandmen, whofe peculiar characteriftic was induftry? A country which was the cradle of every thing ufeful or ornamental that is known among men; and which, under the thorough regulation that might be afforded to it by a Britifh legiflature, would again be reftored to much of its original wealth and felicity. But the neglect of this nation has been fuch, that the fubject has become almoft too great for the attention of thofe, in whofe hands the remedy for thefe evils is lodged. The utmoft that can at firft be done in this great national work, is to

fix

fix right principles, and to eftablifh the
main fupports of good government in India; to fet wife and able men at the head
of our fettlements, leaving the operation
of thofe principles to work its effeets in
the courfe of time. That period will ar-
rive much fooner than the generality of
men expect; for when a gentle, docile,
and induftrious people try out for a good
government, and Great Britain is difpofed to give it, a few years will firmly eftablifh it, if proper perfons be employed
in that great and merciful tafk. Pallia-
tive and temporary meafures will do more
harm than good. The people of that
country have feen the bad effect of waver-
ing and uncertain fchemes, and have not
been induced to increafe the refpect which
we fhould endeavour to acquire from them,
by thofe weak and perplexing meafures.

The main objects of our attention in
endeavouring to perfect the government of
India are the four following:

1ft. To fecure our influence and the
permanency of our eftablifhments there,
by placing ourfelves in fuch a light among
the princes and powers of that country,

as will make it appear beneficial to themfelves to be upon good and friendly terms with us, and confequently will induce them to prefer our interefts, to thofe of any other European nation.

2dly, To revive the internal profperity of the country more immediately belonging to ourfelves, by giving to the natives a permanent inducement to induftry, in cultivating the rich and fertile foil of the provinces they inhabit, which will necef-farily be followed by an increafe of manu-facture, and that again by an increafe of revenue.

3dly, To eftablifh fuch a confolidated body of civil government, as fhall preclude diftraction, diffention, and that fluctuation of counfels which has been fo pernicious and difgraceful, and by this means to give promptitude and dignity to our proceedings there on all occafions.

4thly, To eftablifh a mode of adminif-tering juftice, among the Europeans, and fuch of the natives as may be engaged with Europeans in fuits at law, or who may be guilty of crimes, better adapted to that country than has hitherto been done.

I.

I. The fecurity which the princes of India will place in the juft and equitable conduct of this nation towards them in time to come, will depend entirely upon the intentions which they fhall find exprefled in the acts of the Britifh Parliament. The veil is taken from before their eyes; and they who imagine that the Indian princes do not perfectly underftand, that the Eaft India Company is the mere creature of a fuperior authority, are very much miftaken. That matter is perfectly underftood, and they are willing to believe that all mifmanagement and oppreffion has arifen from their having only an *indirect* connection with the fovereign power of the ftate, and a *direct* connection with a corporation of merchants, to whom the government of that country has been delivered over; and they have alfo been made fully to comprehend that this company is the creature of the King and the national council. Thofe perfons who have the moft intimate knowledge of that country will all teftify, that nothing could fo effectually reconcile to us the hearts of thofe Afiatic powers with whom

we

we are connected, as a kind of parliamen-
tary faith held out to them for their continuance in their prefent dominions fafe
and undifturbed, and the power of tranf-
mitting them to their pofterity according
to the Gentoo or Mahometan practice.
This fingle circumftance would make the
Englifh nation take root in thofe regions,
fo firmly as not to be plucked up by any
ftrength to be apprehended from Europe.
The eftablifhment of a compact Britifh
Empire there, with an affurance on the
part of this nation that it fhould protect
its neighbours, and maintain each in his
juft rights, would be a meafure which
never yet was thought of as a means of
acquiring permanency to any nation in
thofe parts, and from every account that
can be collected is the great point for
which the powers of India moft ardently
wifh. Were this nation to eftablifh fuch
a *league*, and put itfelf at the head of it,
(as it naturally would be) we fhould foon
have reafon to be fatisfied of having fixed
our Empire in the Eaft upon a certain and
durable foundation. A time of perfect
tranquillity in thofe parts, is the proper
.   time

time to eftablifh this balance of power,
and to take that balance into our own;
hands, to be held for generations to come.:
An example will illuftrate this. Hyder
Ali is confidered as a formidable enemy.
Nothing is better known than that he is ·
fuch from provocation and diftruft; it is
alfo well known that he is not without
apprehenfion from the Marrattoes. His
inclination is to be allied to the Englifh,
yet that beneficial alliance has never been
carried into effect. Thefe two points
therefore are effentially neceffary to our
well-being in India. Firft, that the natives of our own territories there fhould
feel themfelves to live under the authority of the ftate itfelf, and not under an
authority fubordinate to that of the ftate.
Secondly, that the powers of India with
whom we have connections by relations
more or lefs near, fhould feel themfelves
to be allied to the Britifh nation, and not
to the Eaft India Company only. This
will give them a perfect affurance of their
own permanancy, aud will accord with all
thofe ideas which prevail in Afiatic minds.
It muft, I fhould conceive, be a neceffary
                                    confequence

confequence of fuch a conduct as this
that the Princes of India would find their
own intereft in preferving and defending
the fyftem here laid down. But in order
that the good correfpondence between the
Britifh and Indian powers fhould be con-
ftantly maintained, it will be of great importance, that the fuperintending government of our fettlements fhould have proper perfons refident as minifters in all the
courts of India. The French have conftant-
ly obferved this rule, and have given us
great difturbance by their attention to it.
Very able men have been found among
the Company's fervants, and ftill abound,
equal to this tafk in point of knowledge,
affiduity, and addrefs. This would teach
men the art of conducting public bufinefs,
and would recommend them in time to the
moft important offices of the government.

II. The next object of our confideration
is the profperity of the natives inhabiting
the Britifh fettlements, being that upon
which our immediate advantage muft depend, and which will be moft effectually
D

fecured

secured to us by the measures touched upon above. The Britifh dominion in Bengal is 600 miles in length, and 300 in
breadth; the extent of our interefts in the
Carnatic, and on the coaft of Malabar, has
of late years been fo much the fubject of
public difcuffion, that it is known to every
reader with fufficient accuracy; and every
map will point it out. In Bengal the
great fource of the Sovereign's revenue is
the rent of land; it becomes therefore
more peculiarly neceffary to attend
to the internal wealth of the country. In this territory however our mifmanagement has occafioned a very mani-
feft decline in agriculture, in trade with
the reft of Afia (from whence fpecie flows)
and in the manufacture of the country.
Thefe three great fources of wealth muft be
reftored before the fovereign ftate can expect to reap any thing like the advantage
which fuch dependencies might from their
nature afford. This may be effectuated in
a very confiderable degree by one fimple
regulation, namely, by abolifhing the deftructive practice of letting the lands for
fhort terms of years; a practice introduced
by

by the Mahometan conquerors for the purpose of periodical plunder and oppreffion, and adopted by the Britifh after their example.

Neither agriculture nor manufactures, which have a reciprocal connection and effect on each other, can ever flourifh where there is no permanent property; and it has become a maxim even in the Spanifh government in their South American dominions, according to a late elegant hiftorian, that in order to obtain an increafe of people, a furplus of labour, and of every thing dependant upon that furplus, the land ought to be divided into moderate fhares, the dominion over it made compleat, and the alienation extremely eafy. It would be an aftonifhing thing to fee defarts in the fineft foil under heaven, towns and villages abandoned, and the moft wretched poverty prevailing among a people naturally bent to induftry, were not a bad fyftem of internal government, and the want of a permanent intereft in the land, fully fufficient to account for this melancholy phænomenon. The pernicious practice of letting the lands

for

for a fhort fpace of time, gives birth to a
regular gradation of tyranny. The great
farmers underletting their lands to fmaller
tenants, who in the end furnifh all the
food for rapine. All political writers have
obferved, that there is no effort of legif-
lation more arduous, no experiment in
politics more uncertain, than an attempt
to revive the fpirit of induftry where it
has declined. This muft be acknowledged to be indifputably true, and the
application of it to our own cafe fhould
be, that every means fhould be attempted,
to cherifh what remains of that fpirit
which in Bengal has advanced very far in
its declenfion. In order to obviate fo fatal
an evil, the fyftem above-mentioned ought
immediately to be abolifhed, and the lands
ought either to be fold in perpetuity, de-
fcendible or devifeable according to the
Gentoo or Mahometan practice, or let for
very long terms: The effect of this would
foon be felt, and there is demonftrable
evidence of its good confequences; for in
thofe parts of India which are not fubject
to a foreign power, and where this is the
ufage, the moft flourifhing people are
found

found. This is a point fo clear in its own nature, that reafoning upon it cannot make it clearer. If that country is conceived by any man to be an exception to the general rule in favour of the permanency of property, the public will at leaft expect to be made acquainted with the grounds, on which that exception is founded. This has never yet been unfolded, nor has the Company ever entertained any ideas of correcting this practice; and unlefs the legiflature fhall think fit to interpofe, the private intereft of particular officers under the Company will render it perpetual. Reafon, principle, and the hiftory of every other nation concur, in leading us to conclude that a contrary practice would give new vigour to the agriculture of our territories, and would even induce the fubjects of other Mahometan princes to fettle within the Englifh pale. This would draw after it its conftant attendants, increafe of population, of manufacture, and of commerce to the other parts of Afia, which laft ought to be encouraged and promoted, by every means that a wife government can devife; for the quantity of

manufacture

manufacture will ever be co-extensive with the market which invites the sale of it; open a free passage to more extensive markets, and every exchangeable commodity will find its way there in abundance. The investments would also be naturally and necessarily increased in quantity, and decreased in price.

The terms upon which the practice alluded to should be abolished, might be made a means of acquiring a great public stock. A permanent interest in the lands of Bengal, &c. would raise, on the most gentle and equitable terms, *ten millions sterling*, and continue subject to a quit-rent nearly if not fully equal to the present reserved rent. Much hidden treasure, as was observed above, would rise again from the bowels of the earth to be given in return for this permanent property, and it would become the interest of the purchasers to concur in preventing any hostile attempts from the European powers, against the British provinces. Moderate and equitable imposts, in the shape perhaps of an equal and small land tax, and of equal and small duties on merchandise, (excepting

ing always grofs articles to be wrought up in manufactures) might fecure a regular addition of income, exclufive of the quit-rents, which would keep pace with the growing profperity and wealth of the country. Alterations in the ftate of any extenfive territory, which are of the magnitude and importance of thofe here propofed, muft however be cautioufly and gradually introduced. Wherefore it fhould feem to be advifeable, to try the experiment upon a certain portion of the lands, and to be guided by the fuccefs of the experiment in that inftance. Should it be attended with the advantages which every principle of found policy leads us to hope, all the benefits above ftated will neceffarily follow, and no lofs can accrue from having made the attempt. The annual *quit-rent* would be chearfully and punctually paid ; and confequently thofe painful expedients would not be neceffary, without which the rents payable for a fhort and precarious intereft cannot now be recovered. A few officers would fuffice to collect it, a few boards to receive it, and much litigation and difpute between the council

and

and court of juftice would be prevented. Without fuch an extenfive meafure as this, it is demonftrable by figures that Bengal cannot fupport the heavy balance againft her. A large and perpetual wafte pipe muft drain the refervoir, unlefs the means of influx be opened and kept free.

As thefe few pages are confined to general principles only, founded upon that which is univerfally acknowledged by every one acquainted with that country, a proof of the comparative efflux and influx of fpecie into, and out of Bengal, would be tedious and unneceffary, having already frequently been laid before the public. At a future time, when the principles themfelves fhall have been in the hands of the public, particular points may with more advantage be enlarged upon.

III. Having endeavoured to fet forth in a few words the meafures by which our interefts in India are to be placed on a fecure footing, both with refpect to the fovereign powers there, and the native inhabitants of the Britifh provinces; we come now to treat of that form of government abroad,

abroad, which muſt eſtabliſh and preſerve this great national work.

Separate and unconnected governments are in their nature liable to every objection; a contradictory ſyſtem of politics may take place in each of them, and has in fact taken place on many important occaſions, and accordingly the late Eaſt India act has conſidered them as pernicious. A general ſuperintending power ought ever to be eſtabliſhed in diſtant ſubordinate territories, and by parity of reaſon, it may be concluded, that the executive authority of government, placed in ſeveral co-ordinate perſons, will be attended with the ſame kinds of inconvenience. Party, faction, and fluctuation of meaſures, have been found to be inſeparable from ſuch a ſyſtem, as the late revolution at Madras, and the political hiſtory of Bengal during the laſt five years, have proved beyond all doubt. Could one man be found equal in point of ability to the taſk of governing alone, and fit in point of integrity for ſuch a truſt, it would be the beſt poſſible method to a-dopt; but as many reaſons muſt immediately occur againſt that mode, indepen-

E   dent

dent of the difficulty, or perhaps impoffi-
bility of finding fuch an individual, the.
neareft practicable plan muft be adopted.

The precarioufnefs of life in every part
of India, renders it neceffary to guard a-
gainft its fatal effects. For this reafon a
fucceffion muft be provided in every office
political and judicial, and the refidence of.
the fuperintending government may be re-
moved from Calcutta, with great advantage to the provinces, and to the conduct
of public bufinefs. The confideration alfo of the great extent of power which muft
unavoidably be placed in the hands of the
executive authority there, makes it abfolutely neceffary that a ftrong check fhould
be put upon the Governor General; yet at
the fame time it is highly impolitic that
this check fhould be of fuch a nature as
may eventually overpower him. The right
medium has never yet been adverted to,
the confequence of which has been, that
diffenfions have arifen in the fettlement of
Madras, highly prejudicial to the interefts
of this country, and the moft difgraceful
contefts and fluctuation of counfels have
taken place in Bengal. It is a humiliating
confideration

confideration to think that the form of the
government eftablifhed there fhould admit
of fuch degrading animofities, and that
public meafures in thofe countries fhould
in many inftances be decided by the doctrine of three to two, and feven to fix, as
the chances at a gaming table. The individuals have acted on all fides, as men will
ever do in fimilar fituations, namely, according to their private interefts, and as
the infatiable love of gain fhall direct
them. The legiflature at home is alone
to blame, which leaves room for fuch
a childifh train of politics. The natives
may juftly exclaim with the frogs in the
fable, " It may be fport to you, but it is
" death to us ;"—and the Britifh nation
at large may, in a great degree, join in that
exclamation.

The commiffions under which the Governors appointed by the Company have
acted, leave it doubtful among the beft
lawyers of the time, what is the precife
fituation and power of a Governor. Some
conceive him to be a neceffary party in all
deliberations, as the mayor of a corporation ; others, that a majority may over-

rule

rule him, exclude him, and even act
without him, as the Eaft India Company
have determined in their late inftructions
to the Governor and Council of Madras,
contrary to the opinion delivered very
lately from the Bench, on the late trial of
the information directed by the Houfe of
Commons. On the other hand, it has been
contended by a late Governor of Madras,
that he had a negative voice in all matters
of ftate, under his prefent commiffion:
Any one, who will give himfelf the
trouble to inveftigate this queftion, will
fee that there is fome ground for this variety of opinions, arifing from the continuance of that inaccurate form of a commiffion, which was fufficiently explicit,
at a time when the Governor and Council
were little more than a committee of merchants fuperintending the Company's
trade. From hence it is plain that the
nature of a Governor's office muft now be
new modelled, and accurately defined
by the inftrument of his appointment.
The afcertaining of a Counfellor's office
will then be no difficult tafk; but we muft
go much deeper. Nothing is more clear
in

in theory, than that a general fuperintending government is abfolutely neceffary
in India, and in practice it has been found
to anfwer very falutary purpofes, both a-
mong ourfelves, and among the Dutch.
It was a favourite idea of the late Lord
Clive, who knew that country well, and
whofe political fagacity was inferior to no
man's, that the refidence of the general
government ought not to be at Calcutta,
but that it would be placed with more advantage at MUXUDABAD. The benefits
which would arife from this change of the
feat of government, are very confiderable:
The collectors of the revenue would not
then be under the neceffity of coming to
the extremity of the province, in order to
tranfact their bufinefs, and of leaving their
refpective diftricts during their abfence, in
the hands of deputies who fail not to take
an advantage of that circumftance, ex-
ceedingly injurious and oppreffive to their
inferiors. The cabals, intrigues and parties prevailing at Calcutta, which is
crouded with people of every rank and de-
nomination, would in a great degree be
prevented, by placing the general government

ment at fome diftance, and every man would not then enter into politics and party, as has been too much the cafe at Calcutta ever fince the Britifh nation grew to its prefent height in that country.—Another confideration too ought to have fome effect. The climate of Muxudabad is one of the wholfomeft in Indoftan; a confideration which from every reafon ought to weigh very much, and if no irrefragable argument can be urged againft it, ought to be decifive. Much advantage might alfo arife from placing the great executive authority at a little diftance from the familiarity, which in the nature of things muft take place between the Governors and their fubjects, in the great mercantile town of Calcutta; fuch familiarities being naturally increafed by a certain feeling of banifhment, common to all men who find themfelves fubjected to the fame perils, in a country very diftant from their native land. The city of Muxudabad is but twenty-four hours journey from Calcutta; fo that on prefling occafions, the Governor might foon be prefent there, and his difpatches would be little retarded

by

by a diſtance ſo inconſiderable. The Government General has now very little to do
with the mercantile concerns of the Company, as a Board of Trade ſuperintends the
matter of inveſtment; and this obviates the
only objection to Lord Clive's idea, which
was, the neceſſary attendance of the Governor and Council at Calcutta for that
particular purpoſe. All theſe reaſons,
therefore, concur in favour of the Governor's reſidence at Muxudabad, viz. The
comparative wholeſomeneſs of the climate,
the great convenience to the natives, the
abſence from diſſipation, party, and faction, and I may add too, the coincidence
with the prejudices of the country, in ſee-
ing the government eſtabliſhed in the an-
cient place of its reſidence. The Exche-
quer muſt of neceſſity follow the Supreme
Power, but the miniſters of juſtice might
ſtill remain at Calcutta, together with all
other Boards and Officers connected with
the merchandiſe of the Company; and
very ſalutary effects would proceed, in a
variety of reſpects, even from the local ſe-
paration of traffick from politics.

The

The fubordinate governments of Madras and Bombay are by the Act 13 Geo. III. c. 63. fubjected to the Supreme Power, only *in matters refpecting peace and war.* This is undoubtedly a reftriction much too narrow; for it becomes a queftion of nice cafuiftry, what may, or may not be a a matter of peace and war. Thus in the late confufions at Madras, it has been doubted whether the cognifance of that matter did or did not fall within the literal or conftructive terms of the act of parliament, giving coercive authority to the Supreme Council: But it is obvious that a Supreme Government ought to be fupreme in every point. Nothing that is done in any of our fettlements can be indifferent to us, or without fome poffible confequences which may materially affect the general intereft; and as the Supreme Government muft be confidered as a public deputation, intended to regulate the national interefts in the whole of our Eaftern dominions, their authority ought to be without fpecific reftraint or defcription in exercifing the legal power delegated by the nation. This confiftency in government

ment has ever yet been wanting, and the want of it has been regretted by every writer upon the fubject of our affairs in India, as well as by every individual converfant in them; and having been remedied in a very beneficial degree by the late act of parliament, we have every reafon to make that part of the government perfect, by following out the imperfect regulations of that act on this fubject, which were wifely intended to be but temporary, and experimental. The powers therefore vefted in the Supreme Council being circumfcribed by no bounds but thofe which the law of the land impofes, and extending to all perfons, and all places, it becomes a very important point to fettle the conftitution of this fuperintending authority.

It was obferved above, that feparated and unconnected governments were in their nature an impolitic inftitution, and that by a fimilar kind of reafoning, equal or nearly equal authority, vefted in feveral perfons, muft alfo be confidered as impolitic. Hitherto the authority of the Governor, in his capacity of Prefident of the Council, has been confidered by the warm-

F   eft

eft advocates for the extenfion of his power, as giving him only a cafting vote, and a neceflary feat in all deliberations. In a variety of inftances the Governor of Bengal has been in the minority, and has been wantonly teazed and humiliated by the majority: Different parties have by death or other accidents been triumphant in their turns, and government by that means fhamefully debafed. If it be ever intended that the government of India fhould be carried on with vigour and uniformity, it will be neceflary to inveft the Governor with a power of *putting a negative* upon the proceedings of his Council, that Council being always at liberty to minute their propofition when they fhall fee occafion. The practice of corrupting the Council, which has poifoned the whole fyftem of Indian government, will by this means be done away, and a fufficient controul will ftill remain upon the Governor, as he will be under the neceffity of ftating all matters to his council, of hearing every thing ftated by them, and of running the hazard of acting againft the opinion of a majority. Any man who ventures to make

ufe

ufe of his negative power, muft be very well founded in his judgment; nor can it eafily be fuppofed, that he would differ from them, unlefs his reafons for fo doing could well ftand the teft of examination. The queftion refolves itfelf into this. Is it a greater evil, that a Governor fhould have it in his power to put his negative upon the proceedings of his council, than that the Counfellors fhould be co-ordinate with the Governor, fo as that a faction among themfelves, or a fyftem of corruption, fhould enable them to overpower the Governor, and thereby render themfelves objects of bribery, job, and Afiatic intrigue? Experience has fhewn that the latter is the leaft dangerous of the two. The council has ever been the feat of corruption, becaufe they have had a deliberative voice in the adminiftration of government, and could compel the Governor to adopt their meafures. If that deliberative voice fhould be rendered not binding upon the Governor by means of the negative propofed, the beft and moft difinterefted effects of a council will ftill remain, and the price of a counfellor's vote in the Indian market

F 2   will

will be rendered of little or no value. The nomination to all civil and military offices ought from the fame reafons to be placed in the hands of the Governor, fubject to a controul from Europe; for all cabal and intrigue in the councils have fhewn themfelves in thefe appointments. The diffentions at Madras afford ample evidence of this. Who fhould, or fhould not be appointed to fill the higheft ftations at Tanjore, was the queftion which brought to light the diffentions in that fettlement; and it has been fufpected by many (though certainly never judicially proved) that this queftion, apparently trifling, became important to the parties from an undue influence obtained over the majority of the council : Be that as it may, the fact itfelf is a powerful reafon for diminifhing their authority, and giving fome preponderance to that of the Governor. Of late years, accident has often determined in Bengal the hands in which the fupreme authority fhould refide; the inferior fervants of the Company have therefore been capricioufly difmiffed from their employments, and their fucceffors

as

as capricioufly difmiffed, when chance turned the cafting vote the other way. Can fuch a mode of government be either creditable or beneficial to the public ? Experience is the only fure guide in all political regulations, and that experience tells us, that if a Governor be not invefted with fuch a negative authority as is here propofed, a corrupt or caballing council will never be wanting to rule according to their own interefts or caprices. Such a power being vefted in the Governor, it becomes fo much the more important to confider of what defcription that Governor ought to be. It is with fome furprife that we now look back upon the practice which obtained till within thefe few years, of raifing the Governors and Counfellors to thofe high ftations merely by rotation. This might be a juft and equitable practice before the acquifition of a great political intereft in that country, becaufe the management of mercantile concerns is in a great degree matter of experience only; but when complicated political interefts of a vaft empire become the fubject-matter of their truft, very chofen men muft

be ·

be specially appointed to undertake that charge. Even since the passing of the late act of parliament, the ancient predilection seems to have continued in favour of gentlemen who have passed the former part of their lives, and have received their education and habits in that country; and with respect to Madras, (where this has been the case without exception) a great law officer lately threw out in the court of King's Bench, that some persons of that description were now *bidding* for that very government. It is certainly a very illiberal thing to suppose, that every man who has made his fortune in India is unfit to be trusted with the government. Many able and honest men have returned from that part of the world, after having rendered signal service to their country. Men who by a spirit of adventure and great perseverance advance their private fortunes, beginning in an humble station, and rising to a certain degree of rank in the state, are intitled to every degree of respect. All the distinctions of rank in society have begun in that manner, and the prospect of arriving at wealth and honours is the great

stimulus

ftimulus to all fubjects, born to the ne-
ceflity of profecuting fome profeffion in
this country. No man of candour therefore will withhold his approbation of the
honours which have been beftowed on
gentlemen who have made their fortunes
in India, and intitled themfelves to the
notice of their Sovereign. At the fame
time it muft be confeffed, that great and
liberal ideas of government are not moft
likely to be acquired, in the progrefs from
poverty and infignificance to wealth and
power in India. The generality of men
are not fo much influenced by the abftract
principles of moral rectitude, as by fome
powerful fecondary principles of action.
One of the moft confiderable of thofe fecondary principles, is the prefervation of
an eftablifhed character, and the fear of
difgracing our acquaintance, our friends,
and relations. Men too young to have
eftablifhed a fixed reputation in England,
and born in the lefs confpicuous ranks of
life, if they fhall chance to return to their
native country in affluence acquired in India, have then to begin the work of form-
ing a reputation at home ; but during their
refidence

refidence in the Eaft, they have not felt the influence of the motives above-mentioned. They were never deterred from purfuing the favourite object which was early fet before them, by the controul which arifes from the relation they bear to many refpectable connections in England, and the dread of not acting up to the uniform tenor of their lives in their native climate. Having none other than the habits and ideas prevalent in the feat of their early education, they are principally directed by them. When men of a different defcription have been placed at the head of affairs in India, they have ever been found proof againft the contagious avarice and rapacity, which prevail there. The reafon is plain; no price can be found adequate to the mortification of returning to England, and finding a character once unexceptionable, perfectly altered, or even rendered difputable. Accordingly, no man has ever ventured to infinuate the fmalleft degree of reflection, upon the integrity of Sir John Clavering, and Mr. Monfon, who felt that it was expected of them, in a confpicuous ftation abroad,

to

to fupport the honour of their numerous
connections at home, and of refpectable
and noble birth. It ought to be the duty of
a minifter not to accept of the firft and moft
neceffitous volunteer, but to difcover with
fome pains men who are bound by all
thefe confiderations, and to fecure to them
and their families a handfome indemnity
for the profpects which they may relin-
quifh in Europe: Nor is it to be imagined
that fuch men are not to be found, unlefs
we adopt the maxim which is induftrioufly
propagated from that country, that there
is fo much intricacy and myftery in the
affairs of Afia, that a whole life-time is
fcarcely adequate to the comprehenfion
of them. This doctrine has been artfully
and fuccefsfully inculcated ; and yet we
find that a common fhare of good underftanding, joined to much attention and induftry, has enabled fecret and felect com-
mittees of the Houfe of Commons, in no
long fpace of time, to be more mafters of
the fubject, than moft men who return
from the common routine of bufinefs in
the Eaft. We find many individuals alfo
who are very confiderably verfed in Indian

G   affairs

affairs from converfation, correfpondence,
reading, and reflection : And in truth thefe
matters have of late years become fo much
the fubject of public attention, that almoft
every one has gained a competent knowledge of the hiftory, manners, and politics
of that country. There can be no doubt,
therefore, but that a man of education,
with an underftanding turned to public
bufinefs, carrying out with him a general
knowledge of Eaftern politics, would in a
fhort time acquire that degree of local
knowledge, which would render him capable of executing, with infinite advantage
to the public, every meafure which his
good intentions, and the powerful obli-
gations impofed by the pride of a clear reputation, together with the dread of difgracing an honourable parentage, could
fuggeft to him. For thefe reafons, it is
manifeftly a matter of great public confequence, to place fome men of reputation
and connection, from this country, at once
in the higher ftations of the government
in India. It is far from being contended,
that men of the defcription which has been
given, fhould entirely exclude all others,
but

but only to prove that they ought not to be excluded; on the contrary, that without a mixture of such ingredients there can be no good government in that country. It must be owned, that the discovering of the characters here alluded to, is no very easy task, though undoubtedly it may be ef-fectuated. The nature of our free consti-tution, together with the manners which follow from it, and the prospects which it affords, makes it a matter of some dif-ficulty to find men of ability willing to adventure in those distant undertakings; at the same time this very constitution and these manners form a greater number of subjects adequate to such employments, than any others in the world. The field which is opened in England to every de-gree of talents and industry is very large. The profession of arms in the land and sea service, demands a great supply, and the learned professions of divinity and law have their respective allurements. The former offers ample emoluments by means of what is vulgarly called interest, and the latter by means of genius and industry. The number of able subjects seated in either

G 2   House

House of Parliament, and who from that situation are exempted from the necessity of indulging or cherishing the spirit of adventure, or expect so to be, is very large; and these considerations must strongly influence every man so circumstanced, who thinks of abandoning his closest connections for a time, and who runs a risk of falling a sacrifice to the climates of the East.

Difficult however as the task may be, it is certain, that with some degree of pains, and proper encouragement, such men are to be found; or rather it should be said, that men are to be found in the British nation, equal to any possible task where honour is to be acquired, or public service to be done, ready to undertake it. In a case where so deep an interest is at stake, it may reasonably be required of a minister to consider in his own mind, or to be informed from others, of persons adequate to these stations, and to take every means of inducing such persons, when found, to bear that part in the public service: But instead of making such efforts, it has been usual to be satisfied with chusing out of

two

two or three volunteers, who having made one fortune in that country and mif-fpent it in this, are defirous of returning to make a fecond as quickly as poffible.

Many perfons fitted in every view to conduct our diftant political interefts, either defpairing of fuccefs in their applications to thofe in power, or who may not have turned their thoughts to that particular object, would, if it were fuggefted to them, readily accept that fervice. The fame induftry ought therefore to be ufed by the minifters in this country as in France, to caft their eyes on the moft proper perfons, and propofe fuch employments to thofe whom they fhall think the moft virtuous and moft capable. In this refpect the French and other nations have fome degree of advantage over us : For as the opportunities of obtaining a fhare in the adminiftration of public affairs, are not fo extenfive among them by reafon of the want of legiflative affemblies, they therefore have a great furplus of fubjects, able and willing to ferve the ftate in public capacities, in any corner of the globe, and thofe too men of the beft and moft honourable

able families. The honour of bearing the King's commiſſion is ſufficient to induce any ſubject in France to forego for the time his comforts and enjoyments ; the objects of his ambition at home being very few, and attainable with great difficulty. For this reaſon, the French ambaſſadors, governors, and foreign agents of every deſcription, have been found in almoſt every inſtance to have been men of very ſupe- rior capacity and addreſs, and of theſe there has never been wanting a ſucceſſion ; whereas in England, it has been matter of ſome difficulty to find a ſucceſſion of per- ſons fit to conduct the buſineſs of the ſtate with ability in the ſubordinate foreign de- partments, and who are at the ſame time deſirous of being ſo employed, or would ſubmit to the diſguſts which attend all ſo- licitations addreſſed to perſons in office. The forward applications of indigent or preſuming perſons, are generally in ſuch caſes attended to ; and miniſters ſuffer themſelves to be overcome by the ſuperior importunity of ſome one of many impro- per candidates, and exert their influence in the India Houſe accordingly. But they

ſhould

fhould recollect that the character which ought to be fent to our foreign dominions, for the purpofe of placing them upon a fecure foundation, and of introducing juft and enlarged principles of government, is exactly oppofed to that of an importunate volunteer. A man of knowledge, coolnefs, and moderation, will not be a likely perfon to purchafe fuch an appointment at the expence of a follicitation at the Treafury, or the India Houfe: Yet fuch is the character fit to be appointed, and fuch alone can fave that part of our dominions from becoming detrimental inftead of being highly profitable. It were better too that our Governors in India fhould not be permitted to hold their feats in parliament, as that naturally gives them an additional defire to return from their ftation; nor ought they in juftice to enjoy that privilege, if they are nominated by the Crown, when a Governor in our Weft-India fettlements is deprived of it. An Eaft India Governor fo nominated, would indeed by anology, or even a found conftruction of the difqualifying acts, be confidered

fidered as incapable of fitting during the continuance of his government.

Not many years ago the minifters of Spain found it neceffary to confider in their own minds, of fome fit perfons to conduct the goverment of South America, which had hitherto been very ill adminiftered. One man of abilities and integrity, the Marquis de Croix, was picked out for this purpofe, who has rendered more effential fervice to both Old and New Spain, than perhaps any fubject that country ever produced. He returned in the year 1772, with great honour to himfelf, his friends, and relations whom he had left behind him, and with that unfpeakable fatiffaction of mind which arifes from a confcioufnefs of having wrought the utmoft degree of good which his fuperior knowledge, humanity, and parts eminently qualified him to do; and what is more remarkable, with a very moderate addition to his fortune, if he made any addition to it whatever.

- I have dwelt a little the longer upon this particular topic, becaufe it is generally conceived that feveral new appoint-

ments

[57]

ments muſt ſoon take place in that line of public employment: and if this plain ſtate of the miſchiefs which may ariſe from continuing the old ſyſtem of nominating Governors and Counſellors, ſhould accidentally chance to be honoured with the peruſal of any among the principal ſervants of the State, it is poſſible that it may help to awaken their attention to a matter ſo extremely important.

The Governor in each of the three preſidencies ſhould be aſſiſted by a council, not exceeding four in number; and it is obvious that ſome of thoſe ſhould be perſons the moſt eminently converſant in the detail of the country buſineſs. The commander in chief for the time being ſhould alſo be of this body, but the chief *Law Officer* need not have a ſeat at the political Board, but ought however to be conſidered as bound to give his aſſiſtance when required. A council ſo conſtituted, and ſubject to the Governor's *veto*, but at the ſame time at liberty to record their own propoſitions if negatived, and the grounds of their diſſent from thoſe of the

H   Gover-

Governor, feems to comprife in it all the advantages of a controul upon the Governor, and at the fame time of extracting that fting with which they have in many recent inftances fo grievoufly annoyed him, to the great impediment of our national concerns. The councils upon the coafts of Malabar and Coromandel being in all refpects fubject to the Supreme Council in Bengal, ftrength and confiftency will thereby be given to the whole Britifh dominion in India; and thofe deftructive fcenes which have expofed us to the contemptuous hatred of the natives, and the ridicule of Europe, will probably be prevented, or will at leaft be lefs likely to occur than they have been heretofore.

IV. It were to little purpofe to eftablifh a well-connected mode of government in any ftate, or to afcertain by laws the permanency of every man's intereft in his lands and goods, unlefs that government were itfelf controuled, and that permanency of property fecured, by an

2   upright

upright adminiſtration of juſtice ; for this it is, which gives real effect to the wifeſt regulations that human prudence can invent. In this matter the legiſlature has felt itſelf under very confiderable difficulties : on the one hand, they were ſenſible of the great wiſdom of the municipal law of England in the protection of private property, and they felt that the merciful nature of the Engliſh mode of trial in criminal matters makes it applicable to many caſes, whereſoever they might happen to ariſe, being founded in the true and univerſal principles of abſtract juſtice, and proceeding upon rules of evidence, ſcrupulous and accurate to an extreme. On the other hand it muſt be acknowledged, that much of that law, complicated and voluminous as it now is, takes its riſe from the peculiar nature of the Engliſh government, and the manners and cuſtoms of a free people; ſo that in many reſpects no ſyſtem of municipal law can be more local or more peculiarly adapted to the country where it prevails. To tranſplant it, therefore, is a work

H 2

of

of great delicacy, and the good or bad effects of that meafure muft entirely depend on the judicious manner of applying the principles which govern the laws of one country, to another differing entirely in its cuftoms, habits, manners, and fubfifting regulations. A vaft proportion of the technical fyftem of our law, though highly beneficial to ourfelves, would be intolerable to any other people, and even the principles themfelves ought to be felected by a very liberal underftanding, in order to be made applicable to any other people, even in matters of private property. With refpect to crimes, peculiar manners give occafion to a feverity in punifhing, very different in different focieties, according to their deftructive tendency in each refpective fociety. A moment's confideration will be fufficient to convince any man, that an act done in *England*, and attended with the forfeiture of life itfelf, need not perhaps be attended with any punifhment at *Conftantinople*, approaching to that degree of feverity. The crimes which are called *mala in fe*, muft

must it is true be univerfally confidered
as the proper objects of vindictive juftice;
but the inferior claffes, even of fuch
crimes, may differ very much as to their
pernicious tendency in different ftates;
and the *mala prohibita* are in their nature
offences relative to the peculiar fociety by
which they are enacted. The great difficulty therefore confifts in the application of fuch parts only of our law civil
and criminal, as may, from its abftract
juftice, be applied to cafes arifing in a
country differing from our own, and of
reftraining the minifters of juftice from
an improvident application of it in other
parts. It is impoffible to lay down a
precife rule to regulate a judge in this
nice determination. That the law of
England fhould be adminiftered to parties
purely Englifh is liable to no exception,
but, on the contrary, it is the right of
Englifh fubjects in civil cafes, and is what
they have been taught to expect in criminal profecutions. The difficulty com-
mences when we fuppofe one of the natives to be party to a civil fuit, or pri-
foner

foner in a criminal proceeding. The juriſdiction of the Supreme Court of Juſtice eſtabliſhed at Calcutta by the Act of the 13 G. III. c. 63, is extended, with reſpect to the natives, " to all perſons " who are or have been employed by, or " ſhall then have been directly or in- " directly employed, in the ſervice of the " ſaid united Company, or any of his " Majeſty's ſubjects." The number of perſons who fall within the deſcription of being actually employed, or having been formerly employed, in the ſervice of Europeans, is very conſiderable, and this deſcription was for ſome time inter- preted by the Judges to comprehend all perſons connected with the collection of the rents; and alſo to ſuch of the natives as were impriſoned by thoſe collectors. Writs of *habeas corpus* were accordingly granted to public debtors ſo impriſoned. This was found to affect the public re- venue of the country moſt eſſentially, and has at laſt been ſettled by a ſpecies of compromiſe between the Supreme Coun- cil and Supreme Court. Some explicit

rule

rule however is neceffary in this matter, for there are evils to be guarded againft on both fides. The moft obvious feems to be to withhold the *habeas corpus* in cafes of imprifonment for non-payment of rent, leaving the party to his remedy when he fhall have paid it; in which cafe the Judge fhould think it his duty to carry vindictive juftice to an extreme a-gainft the oppreffor. The collector falls within the defcription of the act of par-liament as a perfon employed in the fer-vice of the Company, and is therefore amenable to the juftice of the Supreme Court, in all cafes where he fhall have abufed his authority; and the King's Attorney General in the fettlement might, in all fuch cafes, file an information, with leave of the court, againft the op-preffor. The line of diftinction, drawn by the act above-mentioned, namely, that a native muft have fubmitted him-felf by a contract in writing to the deter-mination of the Englifh Judges, is very juft and proper: But even then, if a Judge fhall conceive himfelf bound by his

oath

oath to adminifter the Englifh law in its full purity, his decifion may not accord with the intention, and habitual meaning of the native party. Much latitude fhould therefore be allowed to any Judge deciding upon a tranfaction arifing in a country, where the laws, habits, religion, and manners, differ totally from thofe of England. He ought, in fuch cafes, to frame his decifions *fecundum æquum et bonum*, and according to the infight he may acquire into the peculiarities of the national ideas, rather than according to any pofitive fyftem. In criminal cafes, the abfurdity or rather cruelty of applying doctrines *pofitivi juris*, without confidering the current ideas of the country in which they are applied, is fo glaring that every man muft perceive it. The tragedy of Nundocomar muft immediately prefent itfelf to every one's mind. A native Hindoo, of great rank and opulence, was indicted for a forgery, contrary to a pofitive ftatute paffed in the year 1728, and was condemned and executed for an offence againft

againſt that ſtatute, committed nine years
before, and which had never been conſidered in India as deſerving of the laſt
degree of human puniſhment, nor even
in England till within forty years pre-
ceding, at which time the frequency of
the offence, and the peculiar danger of
it in this country, made it neceſſary to
rank it among the hundred and eleven
capital crimes, which a ſubject of England may commit, and for which he may
ſuffer in the firſt or ſecond inſtance.
From what has been ſaid it will readily
be acknowledged, that difficulties almoſt
inſuperable occur in the diſpenſation of
Engliſh law to the natives, when they
happen to be one of the parties litigant.
The moſt beneficial inſtitution for them
would be, to leave the Supreme Court at
liberty to act rather as *Arbitrators* than
as Lawyers; in all caſes where natives are
intereſted on the one ſide or the other. The
court will naturally have a leaning towards thoſe principles of juriſprudence
which are familiar to the Judges; and at
the ſame time it will be enabled to give full

I   ſcope

scope to all local and equitable ideas. In all criminal cafes their power of inflicting capital punishments ought to be circum-scribed by the ancient simplicity of our own law. Treason, murder, rape, and wilful burning of houses, were in an-cient time the only capital offences, and these would still be fully sufficient in In-dia. All subordinate crimes are of a magnitude merely relative to the exi-gences of the society in which they have been made capital. Were the parliament of Great Britain now for the first time to begin the formation of a criminal code, it is highly probable that they would not very much exceed the limits here pre-scribed; *a fortiori*, when they are to in-troduce a system of criminal law into the Asiatic provinces, they should confine the catalogue of capital offences within the narrowest bounds. In all commer-cial countries, it is true, that the crime of forgery becomes a serious object of coercion; yet a specific punishment, such as one or two years imprisonment, a public disgrace similar to the pillory, a

2   very

very heavy fine, or a forfeiture of three times the fum, as in the cafe of ufury in England, might have the fame good con-fequences in India, and would be agree-able to the law of all the world. Were the latitude of determination in all civil cafes which is here propofed, left to the Englifh courts of juftice in India, and the offences to be capitally punifhed there, limited to thofe four which were alone thought worthy of death by the humanity of our own anceftors, and were the crime of forgery fubjected to very fe-vere confequences fhort of death, an Englifh court of juftice, governed as far as is poffible by Englifh maxims of law, would be an effential bleffing to the na-tives of that country. At the fame time that fuch limitations are impofed upon the court with refpect to the natives in criminal cafes, and fuch latitude given in civil cafes, it is by no means propofed that the law of England fhould be admi-niftered to parties purely European dif-ferently from what it is in England : they are bound to fubmit to it, they are ac-

acquainted

quainted with it, and revere it, but the
cafe is widely different with refpect to the
Afiatic fubjects. An appeal from the
Supreme Court to his Majefty in council
is effentially neceffary in this cafe, as in
every other of the fame nature, in order
to preferve the uniformity and integrity
of the law, to controul the proceedings
of inferior courts, and keep them within
the line of their duty. As the latitude
which muft neceffarily be given to the
Judge is very extenfive, he muft be made
proportionably refponfible in all cafes of
wilful malverfation. The conftitution of
the Court of Juftice in Calcutta has
fhewn itfelf liable to fome material ob-
jections. It confifts at prefent of four
Judges, a number objectionable from its
liability to equal divifion, and ftill more
fo from its being expofed to altercations
and conteft, of which the inhabitants of
Calcutta have feen the moft indecent
examples. Much difcretion muft be af-
fumed (if it be not directly given) by
any court eftablifhed in that country,
and this will of itfelf beget great varia-
tions

tions in their fentiments: but the moft
material defect has been feen in their
tendency to party attachments. This
has occafioned a perfuafion in moft men
acquainted with Calcutta, that a fingle
Judge with a deputy to affift him, fimilar
to the Chancellor and Mafter of the Rolls
in England, would anfwer the purpofes
of juftice in a more effectual manner;
and that two perfons acting in fimilar
capacities might be afforded to Madras.
The Superior Judge might be confined
to caufes exceeding two hundred pounds
in value, except where they were tried by
confent before the inferior, from whom
an appeal might lie to the Superior
Judge in all cafes exceeding one hundred
pounds. A fpecies of rivalfhip between
the two courts would thus be eftablifhed,
and they would operate in a degree as a
kind of controul upon each other. In
criminal cafes they ought to fit together,
and the Superior might at all times call
the other to his affiftance in civil caufes.

The fame inftitution eftablifhed at Madras would be of infinite fervice to that
fettlement,

fettlement, as the late difturbances very
clearly evince. The interpofition of a
fenfible Judge might poffibly have prevented the imprifonment of the Governor, and the confequences which have
followed from it to all parties, and
would undoubtedly have prevented the il-
legal and unjuft proceedings of the pre-
tended coroner's inqueft, which no man
can read without horror and aftonifh-
ment.

Weftminfter-Hall will not afford four
capable men for each of thefe fettlements, who would be difpofed to remove
into thofe climates, at the advanced period of life which is requifite for the
exercife of thefe folemn functions. The
candidates for the honours and emoluments of that profeffion being in general
not men of defperate circumftances, are
not much tempted to feek their fortunes
in India; and fuch of them as would
naturally attract the attention of thofe to
whom it belongs to recommend them,
have from that very reafon, well-ground-
ed hopes of acquiring a competent fhare

of

of employment in their own country. There will always therefore be a fcarcity of Indian Judges; and it is reported that upon the firft eftablifhment of the Supreme Court of Juftice only five candidates prefented themfelves, to fill the four feats; and as the novelty of that inftitution produced fo fmall a number, it is not to be fuppofed that many perfons will offer themfelves on future vacancies. If the Englifh Bar will barely fupply four Judges, and it be thought proper to eftablifh a Court of Juftice at Madras; it will be neceffary to divide them in the manner above-mentioned, with a direct appeal from Madras to the Privy Council. The fum at prefent allotted to the Supreme Court is 26,000l. a year. This fum might be diftributed between the two fettlements, fo as to afford a very handfome emolument to the chief and fecond Judge of each, by allotting 9000l. to the chief Juftice of Bengal, 5000l. to his deputy, 7000l. to the Chief Juftice of Madras, and 4000l. to the inferior Judge, leaving 1000l. to the officers of the New Court at Madras.

The

The fettlement of Bombay is fo narrow, that no neceffity has yet appeared of giving them an expenfive Court of Judicature. By thefe means, all diffention, altercation, and tendency to party, would ceafe; and if an expectation of fucceffion were held out to the deputies, it would be an inducement to younger men of merit at the Bar to prefent themfelves for thofe two fubordinate ftations. Both Calcutta and Madras would by this regulation be well fupplied, by the fame number of Judges, and at the fame expence that one court only is now filled. It may be thought that fubordinate Judges will not fo eafily be found, when their falary is 5000l. and 4000l. as they will be on the prefent eftablifhment of 6000l. but the great inducement arifing from the hopes of fucceeding immediately to the very high ftation of a Superior Judge, will ftimulate more powerfully, than the difference of falary propofed would difcourage.

We have now touched upon the feveral heads propofed, and have endeavoured to
attract

attract the reader's attention towards the
fundamental points which ought to be
fettled, when the new arrangement of the
affairs of the Eaſt Indies comes under the
conſideration of the legiſlature. The au-
thor's object has been to impreſs the
reader, whether he be a plain citizen of the
State, a Member of Parliament, or Mi-
niſter, with a juſt ſenſe of the vaſt extent
and importance of the ſubject. It has
been attempted alſo to ſhew, that nothing
ſhort of a found and enlarged political
ſyſtem, founded and carried on by ſome
conſiderable men, can ſave our territory in
the Eaſt from being gradually depopu-
lated and exhauſted; and that by the
eſtabliſhment of ſuch a ſyſtem, well carried on, the advantage to this kingdom
would be both great and laſting. It is
very much feared by the public, that no
ſuch extended meaſures will find their
way into the cloſets of thoſe who are to
determine whether the old ſyſtem is in
ſubſtance to continue, with ſlight and
partial amendments, or whether

Immedicabile vulnus
Enſe recidendum eſt ne pars ſincera trabitur.

K   This

This apprehenſion ariſes from an opinion,
that the conſideration of theſe affairs requires time and leiſure, and that few
miniſters are actuated by abſtract principles of policy in the government of
ſubordinate ſtates, but rather by the ne-
ceſſities of the preſent hour.

In the midſt of a dangerous and complicated war, and much diſtracted by the
activity of a warm oppoſition in Parliament, it is feared that our Miniſters will
ſcarcely be able to afford to this ſubject
the attention which it deſerves, or that
they can avoid conceding many points to
the Company, very pernicious to India,
for the ſake of ſome temporary profit.
Every ground, however, for ſuſpecting
their zeal for the proſperity of ſubordinate kingdoms, ſeems now to be unge-
nerous and unjuſt, when we turn our
eyes towards the kingdom of Ireland.
The ſervants of the State will turn their
attention with the ſame humanity, aſſi-
duity, and true political principles, towards the Eaſtern dominions. They
will recollect that ſo favourable an oppor-
tunity as the preſent never can ariſe, to

2   lay

lay the foundation of a lucrative, profperous, and permanent intereft in that part of the world; that the true intereft of this kingdom requires our Afiatic territories fhould be rendered as productive to the fuperior State as poffible, confiftently with a view to futurity, which can only be done by confulting the true *internal* interefts of thefe provinces themfelves. By thefe means the revenue to be derived from their profperity, and their profperity only, muft be greatly augmented, perhaps beyond our moft fanguine expectations; and might be divided between the purfe of the Company, and that of the Nation, as far as refpects the territorial revenue, and the ftock to arife from the fale of a long or perpetual intereft in the lands, as Parliament, upon a full examination, fhall think juft and reafonable.

F I N I S.

www.ingramcontent.com/pod-product-compliance
Lightning Source LLC
Chambersburg PA
CBHW021529270326
41930CB00008B/1170